IMMACULATE PERCEPTIONS

Also by Latorial Faison

Secrets of My Soul

Visit Latorial Faison Online
www.latorialfaison.com

Email the Author
crosskeyspress@aol.com

IMMACULATE PERCEPTIONS

Poems by Latorial Faison

Cross Keys Press

Cross Keys Press
crosskeyspress@aol.com

Copyright © 2003 Latorial Faison

All rights reserved. No part of this publication may be reproduced, stored in a retrieval system or transmitted in any form or by any means electronic, mechanical or otherwise without the prior written permission of the publisher, except in cases of brief quotations in critical articles and reviews.

Printed in the U.S.A.

For
My husband
Carl Jerome Faison

ACKNOWLEDGEMENTS

God is my refuge and strength! Without Him, I cannot exist in any form. I thank God for His presence in my life. Thanks to all who encouraged *Immaculate Perceptions* and made my first book, *Secrets of My Soul,* a labor of love. Jerome, "The Man in My Life," you know that I don't like to do anything without you. I never have and never will! Thanks for your love and two beautiful sons. Carl & Kendall, when you're old enough tell mommy what you think! To Mama, Daddy, and my Grandma Earline, thanks for your support, selling books and for spreading the word in Franklin and Southampton Co. I love you so much! To the greatest mother-in-law in the world, Mrs. Lillie Faison & to a wonderful father-in-law Mr. Faison, thanks for promoting my work to your family, friends and colleagues. Mrs. Adkins thanks for always reading and supporting. Cat thanks for telling friends and everybody at the Portsmouth Shipyard. Nedra thanks for taking books to S. Korea. I miss you. Marlena thanks for keeping me in the spirit of writing! Jamila, Nia, Monique, Kamili, Jawanda, Tiffany, Odette and Sonya thanks for your friendship and support. Thanks are also due the following: Blackie, Red, Shake, Blondell, Man, Angela, Karen, Esther, Silk & Hulk, Melendez & Rusty, the Bryants Baptist Church family, Rev. and Mrs. Anthony Ferebee, the Shiloh Baptist Church family, the faculty and staff at Southampton High School & Southampton Middle School, Walter Cecil Rawls Library, Travis & Deborah, everybody at Deb's Hair Studio, Judy & Robin at Judy's in Killeen, soldiers in the 502d PSB who have read my poetry, The Happy Bookseller, Angela Bishop & family, Gwen Gibson, Violette, Terri, Philip, Broad Street Books, Spark, Aunt Jean, Aunt Rebbie & Uncle Samuel, Wendell & Andrea, Lelia & Shelia, Uncle RC & Aunt Janice, Jackie Lewis & family, Janice Nance, Evelyn Carter, Mary Ann, Charlie & Gladys, Fat Man, HASTINGS, R.A.W.SISTAZ Book Club, C & B Books, Nathan Lewis, Pam Jarmon, Shonell Bacon, JDaniels, Steven Manchester, Victoria at Skyline Publications and Linda Dominique Grosvenor, James Lisbon, Cynthia Highsmith-Hooks, Dr. Patsy Joyner, The G.R.I.T.S. Reading Club, The D.O.E. Network, Rudy at NathanielTurner.com, Midwest Book Reviews, Alphonza Graham, Salomebey, students & colleagues at CTC, and to the countless significant others not mentioned by name, thank you from the bottom of my poetic heart. You all have inspired me to continue writing, and I look forward to bringing you more! If

Contents

Part One

Haiku 11 (*our relationship*) 13
Immaculate Perceptions 14
And I Thought I Was Free 15
Tango With the Art 16
Knowing You 17
Bring Yourself to Smiles 18
The Greatest Good 19
Final Moments 20
New Places 21
Simplicity 22
Surreal and So Divine 23
Another Cross to Bear 24
In God We Trust 25
In the Midst of it All 26
A Jazz Thing 27
What the Bluest Eye Can't See: *for Pecola Breedlove* 28
Nobody But Nikki 29
Adoration and Praise 30
A Poem for Langston Hughes 31
The Sounds of Blackness 32
I Remember You Dr. King 34
Black Queens 35
What Blackness Brings 36
Everyday Smiles 37
Enemies Within 38
Baby Girls 39
Haiku 12 (*for Carl & Kendall*) 40

Part Two

We're Human   41
Too Fast   42
Children Scorned   43
Again   44
I'm the Kind of Girl   45
Be a Man   47
Merry Men   48
They Call   49
You Taunt Us   50
Two Dollar Bill   51
More than Real   52
Haiku 13 (*problem solved*)   53
Melody of Love   54
A Single, Solitary Moment   55
Yesterdays' Room   56
Solitude   57
Have I Given You   58
My Disease   59
Unequally Yoked   60
Poet*icide*   61
Shop Wal-Mart For *Life*   62
Charades   64
Rights of Passage   65
A Pharaoh's Heart   66
Haiku 14 (*when life is so uncertain*)   67
Making Room   68
If I Taught You   69
You Taught Me   70
Wishes for Grandfathers   71
It Spoke to Me   72
Revelations   73
Restoration   74
Twenty-nine   75
Adam Where Are You   76
I See You   78
Thinking Back   79
We're Falling   80
A Yard of Beauty   81

Part Three

A Blue Moon   82
Choir Members   83
The Big Church   84
Dreams and Things   85
Another Fall From Grace   86
Life After Love   87
The Deepest Part of Me   88
Haiku 15-19 (*epiphany*)   89
Too Young to Sip   90
A Poem for Mama   91
A Phone Call   92
Schooling   93
On Marriage   94
God's Wrath is Coming Down   95
Death   96
Things That Bring Us Home   97
Reasons: *for Miles, Madison & The Rest*   98
The World is Coming to an End   99
Haiku 20 (*trifling*)   100
Afghan Woman   101
Chaos   102
C Words   103
Dying in My Sleep   104
Girl Interrupted   105
My America   106
You'll Never Find You   108
Sacred Places Turned Inside Out   109
Sudden Feelings Never Lasting   110
Deliverance II   111
Not My Nation, Not My Beliefs   112
Where to Now America?   113
The Man in My Life   114
Haiku 21 (*book review*)   115

Part One

HAIKU 11
(our relationship)

words, they approach me
with splendor and pleasantry
then leave my life stunned

IMMACULATE PERCEPTIONS

People read books for different reasons and those close to me will read this in hopes of finding something, perhaps a

revelation of some inherent good or evil coursing through the confines of my mind but I'm not sure what they'll believe after

this read. Maybe you'll find that you have found words with which to speak or maybe you've found a secret place to come

and vent about the things and people you most relent. I don't really know, but these are my most immaculate perceptions which

are given. These are things, places, people and situations as I've seen and known them from moments of encounter and seconds of silence, those that

mean most to our internal thinking and astute personalities. These are just my moments, my thoughts, my simple and immaculate perceptions.

AND I THOUGHT I WAS FREE

You tell me that my words
these words, black words
offend you
but perhaps they bring fear
to a faulty comfort zone
and I will not waste time
wondering why
because poetry is... an experience

your words,
your existence,
your experience

why should mine be any different?

my words,
my existence,
my experience

just me, a black woman
and I thought I was free

just words
and I thought they were free

just writers
and I thought we were free

but apparently we may never be
so long as it pains you
to hear me, read me

while I speak and write poetically

on being black and being me
a black woman
and I thought I was free.

Tango With the Art

Days have no understanding
   of my life
and night is just ordinary
   darkness within me

for the elements of God
   have taught me well
to linger in the shadows
   where realism abides

earthen vessels melting
   wander about cultivating time
and I, in my self-contentment,
   tango with the art of rhyme.

Knowing You

I guess I was about twenty-two
when I realized that you were the most real
black man I'd ever laid eyes on, and I remember thinking
how it was too bad your son didn't inherit
many or any of your best qualities.

If one could ever be both poor and rich
at the same time, then I was because what you lived
to give was worth more than anything I could ever
want or need. Your love and your lessons came
on silver platters.

You're the man, the icon of reality in all of those
books I've shelved housing the prosperity of black men
who have come into their own with very little, and yet
you have given so much to souls in your community,
country, neighborhood, kids whose parents were scarce.

It's a shame the way things really get gotten, but
there's no scandal in being true to your spirit man and
speaking in tongues that babes can understand
because they'll take it all the way to Zion, remembering
always . . . the pleasure of knowing you.

BRING YOURSELF TO SMILES

You've been walking around
with a fool's goal in your pocket
because somewhere down the line
somebody tainted your talents
painted your personality
and gave you a style.

This thing's got you confusing
life and death, satisfaction and wealth
because somewhere down the line
somebody misread your palms
sabotaged the love in your arms
and made it worth your while.

It's a horrible thing to be left undone
to forsake the call in the name of fun
because somewhere down the line
somebody will hand you a revolver
tell you it's a problem solver
and leave you in self-denial.

But here and now is where you are
with a challenging chance to knock it
because somewhere down the line
your true self will have to be defined
take pleasure in the power of personality
and bring yourself to smiles.

THE GREATEST GOOD

Someone important once said
"To whom much is given much is required"
and someone who thought he was important
often quoted Him
while lecturing me about how to live my life
as pious people sometimes do.

I say there's nothing wrong with quoting the Bible
and great philosophers and their profound methods
so long as you're practicing what you teach and preach
for everybody should know by now
that the best illustration is an example
the greatest example is to illustrate
with leadership
following the Prophetic
the profound philosophy
the methodology
to live by it.

Repetition is good and quite effective
but even college professors frown on REDUNDANCY!
"Use examples" say the Lords and Ladies of Arts & Letters
not just advice for writing college papers
not just for higher learning
but for higher living.

There's a lesson to learn everyday
in savoring the sweet
while capitalizing on realizing the essence of
the mistake
the lives we live can lead us
to meaning,
to dreaming
to being
the greatest good.

Final Moments

Will we know our final moments
and breathe as though we've never known
the precious gift of pure air
from minute to minute
each day of our passing lives?

Was I truly leaving this world
the moment I entered
as doctors and philosophers
have so argued and chronicled
in mountains of research?

I'd like to know the day before
and still have the strength to knock on doors
just to say . . . in my way
let every heart "seize the day."

Let my spirit rise to that occasion
memorializing all the love I've ever known
before I leave this place for my eternal home
with family and friends to bid farewell
I'd leave them all a story to tell.

For life in all of its uncertainty
is meanwhile laced with choices
and oftentimes my soul's loudest noise
is made in complete silence
pondering on life's final moments.

NEW PLACES

I keep coming to new places
in my life where I'm continually
forced to find . . . to search for
and hunt for pieces of me.

I'm forced to either fit a mold or not
to survive the change or drop
each time I face the mystery
of new places.

New places breed new people
a continuation of good and evil
but I'll shun misery . . . for destiny
lies in the unfamiliarity of new places.

I will learn the highways
attend the soirees
sit back and watch God
pave and plow the snow days.

Nothing to expect or hope to find
except the confines of peace of mind
and to seek wisdom's many faces
as I wander about in new places.

SIMPLICITY

Too many thoughts to think about in a day
often the soul in me can't decide the flavor of my own cool-aid
simple choices, simple dreams
what they bring, sing and mean
complexity in life's most simple things.

We walk spiritual lines of eschatological and trendy times
not knowing what our fates and forgivings be
in a world that boasts of precious light to see
but runs like those fleeing hell's
fires from beckoning beams
in telltale tunnels and surgical dreams and things
where we sleep, meet and ultimately retreat
some of us.

Trying times breed hearts that lie
while in the heat of daylight's serenading sun
there awaits a warmth that proves dangerously fun
and eyes don't see faults in the fascination of flames
the true end all, be all . . . lives lost in vain
but occasions do arise to greet a stillness in the night
while we, without caution, embark on simplicity's plight.

SURREAL AND SO DIVINE

In search of something
surreal and *so* divine

hearts, minds and souls lie in waiting
prostrate to the skies
beckoning strength, power and knowledge
to make sense of a brand new day
where living and loving
can't help being the same . . . in vain
we proclaim and profess to know
the difference, the distance and deliverance

in search of something
surreal and *so* divine.

Another Cross to Bear

Calamity unfolded,
and the inhumanity of man showed its ugly face
misused America's way for evil and shed our country's blood
murdering hearts and souls
in complete innocence and cold calculation.
The inhumanity of man constructed this deadly plan
for reasons unutterable and insane
to stalk us as we live the mundane.
What a cruel day to ascertain?
Terror left some weeping and others waiting
in a country passionately praying that peace will come.
pure devastation in Manhattan, Pennsylvania and D.C.
how could this horrific tragedy come to be
this dreadful storm we hoped never to see
but a warpath arises from the disastrous dust
someone blatantly took advantage of the kindness in US
from a distance they claimed American life
wreaking havoc on freedom and bringing strife
unsurprisingly the devil hides his irreverent face
thought he'd left each scene without a trace
but the Judgment of God will bring justice, not revenge
may this beastly evil be removed from men
God bless us all, every heart everywhere
as humanity faces tragedy
another cross to bear.

In God We Trust

on wandering wings
and pleading prayers
we seek a comforting end

yet comfort may not
be time's way
of bringing justice to men

remembering the sad day
discomfort and terror
tomorrows to no avail

can't heal the hurt
of a country's earth
bloodied and fatally felled

a massive call to arms
the country's been unsettled
by terrorist attacks

who would have thought
in all the world that four planes
could be hijacked?

victims be gone
to a better place
ascend you from the dust

appear six thousand pennies more
. . . from Heaven
to say "in God we trust"

IN THE MIDST OF IT ALL

In the midst of it all
beautiful America suffers loss
and we are left with the inevitable
. . . taking up another cross.

In the midst of national pain
there is still an axe to grind
a cause to carefully claim
. . . innocent victims to find.

In the midst of it all
the scope of sudden sorrow
there's prospective peace and comfort
in the arrival of tomorrow.

In the midst of the world's wildest chaos
strong souls steadily survive
to lead a nation from diabolical dust
its dying heart to revive.

In the midst of it all
we have a joint cross to bear
in the midst of sacrificial moments
can freedom count on you to be there?

A Jazz Thing

I got a thing
a jazzy blues thing
a bee-bopping
heart throbbing
jazz thing
coursing through my veins

feel me
can't you see
this vibrant vibe in me
leery lookers . . . take a peek
a blues thing . . . a jazz thing
surrounding me

melody . . . melodically
moving me . . . shaking me
the up and down
of a Coltrane sound
where life takes me
rhythmic destiny

bee bop
get your bee bop
do wop . . .
get your do wop
get your groove on
it's a blues thing . . . a jazz thing.

What the Bluest Eye Can't See
for Pecola Breedlove

I wish I could breathe into your spirit
a love that's black
a love that's purely and truly sweet for you

I wish you love
self love
good love

your brown skin is beautiful
your eyes don't have to be blue
just true

character
yours has opened eyes
and revealed shades and shades of blackness

we've got to be who we are
and who we are is black

straight hair and blue eyes are characteristics
but never will they become the character
which makes us who we're destined to be

not even the whitest white can make us pure
not even the bluest eye can make us see it

Pecola Breedlove . . . that's how God made us

and this is what you leave us
 . . . on being black.

NOBODY BUT NIKKI

Every now and then
somebody gets Nikki to sit down and be Nikki
after all, she does it better than anyone else ever could

nobody but Nikki.

I love to read her straight up poetry
her "this is life" interviews
and feel that I've learned just a little more about
my own self, my own life, my own struggle
from reading her and wading in her wisdom

it's great that one could live and love so freely
her thoughts and words flowing as naturally
as waters do in wells and springs
and each time we stop to drink and taste of her
poetic sweetness and realism we are renewed,
refreshed and reliving a missing past
and we walk away energized.

nobody does poetry like Nikki does life
with her *Black Feeling, Black Talk*
she passes down to us a tradition of
poetry and beauty
a boldness with which to speak our minds
to write freely of our times.

nobody but Nikki.

Adoration and Praise

I think of you collectively and simultaneously
the rising and setting of female poetry's sun you are
. . . with your warm words, your giving of light and hope
of new dawns, new days, new life

Nikki you shine on us with beams of beloved verse
and passion setting sister girls in action
to live this thing we call life in the midst of
adversity, storms and mishaps
we remember the humility you bring to black girl worlds
we do . . . remember you

Maya you fall fresh on us like words of God
it's true . . . poetic anointing is what you do
with your causes and clauses
with your words and wisdom
we take the beauty of poetic endings with us
to rest, to sleep, to dreams

You're those sisters we'll always need
to tell us sad and resilient stories
from within and without as we flow back and forth
from Nikki to Maya, from Maya to Nikki

If I could have you both inside my world,
my day, my space, face to face
but for a moment . . . there'd be no talking
no interview, no asking you
how to do a thing . . .
no recitation of verses, no praises, no applause

Just the admiration of the muse's cause
a beautiful and glorious entity
the rising and setting of a sun
something that I'd call . . . adoration and praise
a literary grace that only God could give
a poetic peace so tranquil and new.

A Poem for Langston Hughes

If you could hear me
I'd say "you have your own stamp"
yes, you have been honored with
a United States postage stamp Langston

I just wish you were alive
to see it, to place it on the
upper right hand corner of
a letter to your mother

she who spoke of climbing stairs
not made of crystal, but with splinters
and hard places in them, she who nourished
your dreams and ideas into success

you have written and we have read
the lyrics of your beautiful
and soulful poetic testimonies
of life as you knew it

that you could leave us with the richness
of words on papers and in books
it was an honorable chance that you took
to write to us and tell your story

that we might reign in our seasons
with poetic power and glory
to walk a while in your shoes
and envision the world through your eyes

THE SOUNDS OF BLACKNESS

In my heart there lies no defeat
But in my bosom a triumphant and rhythmic beat
And while my spirit dances with gladness
I am quick to recall the sounds of blackness.

I hear the moaning and the wailing
Of native Africans held captive on ships sailing
As though it were my youth of yesterday
Whispering truths to ears in dark dismay.

The long, persistent motherland call
Of anxious hope and justice for all
As though it beckoned from higher heights
I hear the songs of steal away nights.

That disdainful whip, the startling crack
The sound of fifty lashes to my brother man's back
We listened to hate's hypocrisy, it's rhetoric on religion
And prayed for deliverance complete with wisdom.

I hear Harriet's footsteps and her hushing sacred sounds
As she walked without fear in search of freedom's grounds
To lead as many captives safely to northern light
Her savvy spirit vowed to never give up the fight.

The sighs of relief at a kingdom finally come
Freedom at last for us, the worst of sins to some
But to the surprise and shock of a divided nation
Came the lyrics of a long overdue slave Emancipation.

The endless cheering must have been loud
While those who stood free made their ancestors proud
And the old African's dream really did come true
In a nation where his people were brought to be subdued.

Dr. King shouted "Free at last, free at last . . . "
And his dream of a promised land did come to pass
The sit-ins, the marches and the demand for equal rights
Were necessary for those freed in darkness and deprived of light.

So, in my daily living, I do not dare ignore the sounds
But am honored that my ancestors were *strong* and *freedom bound*
When fellowmen can't remember the truth about this sadness
Pause to share with them one of the many sounds of blackness.

I Remember You Dr King

I remember you as Martin King
You fought to show a segregated world
What peace and unity could bring.

I remember you as Brother Martin
You fed us food for thought
When a dreadful past left us starving.

I remember you as Reverend King
You broke down barriers of ignorance
And gave us songs of hope to sing.

I remember you as Leader of Freedom's Fight
Your preaching and nonviolent teaching
Brought us prayerfully proud into a glorious light.

I remember you as The Dynamic Drum Major
Who marched on Washington and from Selma
That we, as a people, might reap the fruit of our labor.

I remember you as Martin Luther King, Jr.
You salvaged souls of slavery's past
And told us that God would grant "freedom at last."

I remember you as The Man with a Dream
You endeavored to show a world of hate
What brotherly love could really mean.

I salute you Dr. Martin Luther King
For living and dying to set a people free
And for leaving us the legacies of a beautiful dream.

BLACK QUEENS

Look at one another and see the beauty of rainbows
Give your sisters a lasting love to grow
Go back in time . . . feel the pain of matriarchs in the struggle
Who learned to kneel and learned to pray in the times of trouble
The prey of white male predators, handmaids to white females
We sacrificed our bodies and our lives if all else failed
We had no freedom, no voice with which to speak
No peace of mind, no virginity to keep
Sold away from helpless children, taken from our kindred men
We had, who else in all the world, but the Lord to befriend
He heard our cries and pitied our groans
And lead us safely to our present thrones
Our foremothers left us Comfort from above
So live on black queens in unity and in love.

What Blackness Brings

What blackness brings
. . . in the beginning

I was about five years old and I wondered
whether the white folks my grandmother
cleaned for were actually doing us a favor.

Twenty-four years later . . .

My grandmother does not work for them
anymore, but she still serves as a close friend,
and a white man still signs her paychecks.

Two degrees later . . .

I've worked with white folks, worked for black folks,
had paychecks signed by the best of them because of
both favor and fate.

In the end . . .
this is what blackness brings.

Everyday Smiles

I think we all wish that if for but once
the world would look upon us and smile
at our inner beauty, our surprisingly engaging intelligence
our utter uniqueness, our epitomizing essence of being.

I think it would be the greatest thing
a most sincere and tantalizing tribute
if the world could smile just once at us
just because we're thinking and feeling
living, loving and breathing life
because we've felt the frothiness of folly
in sixty seconds of a melting minute.

It would be gigantic, grand, and glorious
a great moment come to pass.

If only the world would smile at us
in our simplicity, in our rare forms
our everydayness, the madness, sadness
and gladness of spirits within
who thrive on the when's and ifs
of everyday smiles.

Then the journey just might be complete
and worth our while because somehow
achievement, hope and acceptance are found
in the two to four seconds
of everyday smiles.

Enemies Within

Sometimes we're to blame
    for our own misery and shame
because we fail to recognize
    that beauty is not fame.

It took years and freedom fights
    for us to see our names in lights
but yet we're the enemy within
    that keeps us from gaining new heights

It's a sadness rooted in the soul
    that tells us we'll never fit the mold
and because we're jealous to a sin
    the ultimate we can't behold.

Often we stand as women and men
    but without the faith to carry or defend
for this is a mighty sadness for us
    that we're often the enemies within.

Baby Girls

It was odd that she would confide in me
she didn't even know me
but I was the first person she'd see
as she sobbed and yelled "They tricked me!"
someone had taken her baby
I couldn't calm her, keep her or reach her
because she was high and beyond reach
my heart was made heavy and soft
like red putty in a preschool playroom
and she couldn't be still, she wouldn't
because they'd taken her baby
and I really didn't know of whom she spoke, at first
"They took her" she cried
and I, myself, had tears in my own eyes . . .
and this lady, this grown girl, this baby
was disheveled and had entered my
Monday morning world
from where she couldn't climb down
sniffing, hyper and breathing hard
with blood shot eyes and crazed cries
she floated away from me
she couldn't come down
she had lost her baby
she let the drugs take her up
and she didn't pass the test
-- clean urine in a cup --
she couldn't keep her baby
she couldn't keep herself
she couldn't love her baby
she couldn't love herself
and there was no one else to blame
for the misery and shame
except tiny traces of crack cocaine
creeping through her veins
although she could feel the pain of love
there was nothing given or gained
just a sad, sad day
for baby girls.

HAIKU 12
(for Carl and Kendall)

I couldn't love you more
for your smiles are laced with a
love so genuine

WE'RE HUMAN *Part Two*

Because we're human . . .
that's the reason we so often go astray
but if and when God brings out the supernatural in us
then we're more than life
more than good
more than human
we are like Him
withstanding and enduring the temptations
in human flesh
but saturated in the supernatural
hiding in Heavenly havens
tenaciously twisted over time
into a perfect peace seeking paradise
even when the ways of this world have ceased to exist
and exalt us into extremes
we live to love it so . . .
that each and every time we break the binds
or fail to feel the flow of life and living
we always come back
to the haunting and half faced fact
that we're human . . . because we're human
so what are we?

Too Fast

With quickness
the world moves too fast for us
running, racing, rear ending us all
into eternity and we,
often without words to speak,
reach daily upward and all around
grasping reality, I think
but our hands and arms return
often empty and unfulfilled
as void as kind words
spoken to the damned
so think, feel and fathom
the fruit of this labor
and be convinced that
with quickness we'll be caught up
remembering our sin and sorrow
as the world moves too fast for us
into tomorrow.

CHILDREN SCORNED

I have not forgotten you
lady at the corner store
you looked at me presumptuously
and swore up n' down you knew more.

I have not forgotten you
with your fickle grin
your kind words and gestures
just another imaginary friend.

I have not forgotten you
because our kind don't forget
children scorned the day they're born
grow up to be keepers of the debt.

Again

She'll never understand the high you get
from leaving her in the dark
to walk and talk inside your head
is like dancing to no rhythmic beat
She sits so still and quiet
that she can hear her own thoughts speaking to her
while biting her bottom lip until it bleeds
because you've done it again
and the love's just evaporating
like water on a sunny day
a year's worth of happiness . . . every second
slips away
while you don't call to say
by midnight
there'll be no love left at all
just her
wondering where you are
where you've been
and most importantly
why she let this happen
again.

I'M THE KIND OF GIRL

I'm the kind of girl you owe an apology
if you think you're going to walk away with the best part of me
because I'm a giver of love, time, talent and vision
and hurting you and teasing you is not my vision
so come close, real close . . . and you will see
that I'm the kind of girl you owe an apology.

I'm the kind of girl you owe an apology it's true
. . . because you walked out on my life, perhaps
the best part of you. I could never ignore my blood
running through even the tiniest vein, but you left me
like forgotten baggage on a midnight train
just come close, real close . . . and you will see
that I'm the kind of girl you owe an apology.

I'm the kind of girl you owe an apology
if you insist on contaminating my world for eternity
because I'm no nonsense, no drama and no juice
I pity the soul whose ignorance runs loose
so come close, real close . . . and you will see
that I'm the kind of girl you owe an apology.

I'm the kind of girl you owe an apology you'll see
because I'm not down with the lies and the trickery
don't misuse your hands and play on my innocence
then twenty years later say you didn't know the difference
just come close, real close . . . and you will see
that I'm the kind of girl you owe an apology.

I'm the kind of girl you owe an apology
if you think bitch is *my* name when you call me
because I have a name, a first and a last
and if you didn't know, all you had to do was ask
so come close, real close . . . and you will see
that I'm the kind of girl you owe an apology.

I'm the kind of girl you owe an apology right now
because I don't easily shake feelings of being let down
I'll forgive you, forget you and try to make the best of you
because life's too short to be angered by the mess you do
but come close, real close . . . and you will see
that I'm the kind of girl you owe an apology.

I'm the kind of girl you owe an apology
if folks think they'll ever get the best of me
because my heart and soul are set in steel
emitting a spiritual resilience that just won't chill
so come close, real close . . . and you will see
that I'm the kind of girl you owe an apology.

BE A MAN

To be a man is to show the world
that you can . . . be a man.

I never thought I'd see it
    the day you'd pack up and give in.
I never thought there'd be a time
    when you didn't want to be a man.

It takes a man to be a man
    to lead a man to read a man
to bring a man to train a man
    to tame a man to be a man.

Take care of business and have a plan
work hard, stay honest and be a man.

It's independence and leadership
    the success of having planned.
It's ideas and creativity
    simply put, just be a man.

It is a man who grooms a man
    to be a man to challenge a man
to stay a man to serve a man
    to complete a man to be a man.

It's visitation and restoration
    revolution and salvation.
It's the principle and where you stand
    so go ahead . . . be a man.

They think they'll never see it
    the day you stay and weigh in.
They think there'll never be a time
    when you will be a man.

It's in you, outside of you,
    all about you . . . understand.
The essence of your life requires that you
    just be a man.

Merry Men

These leather lovers see in black
In smooth grooves across the back
Wherein there lies no slip or slack
Just beautiful, beautiful skin.

Belts, purses, coats and chairs
Fill the room, throughout the stairs
In this joint where no man cares
But loves to live the fit in.

Such ways of life bring us to frowns
Some say it's out of religious bounds
That the God of life will make His rounds
With this merry group of men?

They Call

They call
and sometimes she answers
just to see if they'll stop
and stare into the pupils
of her ideals, her flushed face
and see her for what she is
an approximation of the calling
nothing more, nothing less
she stands midway the aisle
of virtue and femininity
... and they never do
see past her flaws or faults
but leave her lavished with scars for life
that heal and stay within
but they do call.

You Taunt Us

You taunt us
with your steal away smiles
when they're not looking
and I declare there's something
some little part of us that likes it
while most of us call it
the sin it is
while you keep right on
as if one day your style
might just set our souls free
with your words, your eyes
and your come over here smiles
but it wouldn't be worth our while
to open up and receive
the love your kind of living breeds.

Two Dollar Bill

I hope for the best that little old life can breathe
into my sassy spirit . . . sweet and bellowing want for you.
The two-dollar bill has always fascinated me
but it never could buy me much,
and sometimes you just do not give me love
in the midst of my million dollar smiles for you.
I suppose I'll take this notion to my grave,
the unknowns of true love and how it behaves.
So spin a satirical song of sentiment into my soul
and I'll memorize the melody methodically
and reenact your rhythms . . . replay your rhymes.
I'll sing your synonymous song to sleep
each time it seems that your love has left me
feeling foolishly fascinated by the inadequacy
of a two dollar bill.

More Than Real

The surprise in my eyes is fake
hiding behind a two year old truth
I said I wouldn't say it
"I told you . . . "
You're just too damned good.
No tears. No time. No reparations.
It's too late for love now.
My eardrums have crazy conversations
because they remember your voice
and they, too, recall the choice you made
because it was simple and sincere
you couldn't fake it because you couldn't lie to love
but this time you're being big about it
and though the surprise in my eyes be fake
this time . . . you are more than real.

HAIKU 13
(*word problem*)

It's mathematics
when I subtract you from me
and I equal love

Melody of Love

You come by me
like a Virginia breeze
a benevolence that cools my soul
to satisfaction and leaves me waiting
for the next wind to come.

I wait earnestly for the day
of your promised rapture
because I know well the knowledge
you bring to my world
making the living worthy.

To think that you're essential
to my reality just radiating
the warmth of sun into my being
embedding blessed behavior in me
as God condones my conscience.

So live in the lining of my soul
play proudly upon my heartstrings
that we might melt into a melody of love
laboring long because it sounds sweet
and brings peace to a dream.

A Single, Solitary Moment

Sometimes
it's as if salvation begins and ends with it,
the calming reassurance of a single, solitary moment
with you.

Trees sway swiftly to the rhythm of breezes blown
by the breath of you, and I say to myself "what's a soul to do"
but bask in the glow of your presence revealed and allow the
straddling spirit in me to be healed time and time again.

This head of mine is not equipped to fathom
why such infinite joy you bring
or the origins of the spiritual in songs we sing
but holding on to what a harvest is
I watch a seed planted grow into something plentiful
and I am amazed to the power of infinity
beyond the confines of sense, time, the man
and the muse.

For sometimes
it's as if salvation begins and ends with it,
the calming reassurance of a single, solitary moment
with you.

YESTERDAYS' ROOM

At times the room was
very small, moist and musty
but it worked well for us
and was luxurious for love making
and one on one scrabble games.

Seven years of weekends
staring into the screen of a
late 1970's floor modeled TV
and three semi charismatic
channels of game shows,
late night entertainment,
the 6 o'clock news . . . it was
the country life.

And the VCR mama bought
one Christmas, one she paid
almost five hundred dollars for
in the early 80's, was our ritual
escape into other worlds of city
and night life, rated R movies,
cussing, fornication and the like.

It was essential time
in a special and obviously necessary room,
the beginning of who we were
and the dusty prospect of what
we might ever become.

Now more than seven years
away from the close encounters
of that little room that held us close
as we held each other innocently
in teenage love and laughter

We reflect on good times
spent in close quarters
a place not really our own that
really was . . . so as to keep us
remembering the beauty and importance
of yesterdays' room.

SOLITUDE

We walked inside
to see no one else
but us
stand and stare
at each other's glare
in the 9th floor sliding glass doors
silence
a sound we had not fathomed
in three years
and some kids ago
we had to take this one
nice and slow
a week of oneness
solitude.

Everything a creamy shade of blue
genuinely gold trimmed
recessed lights
romantically bright
yet enticingly dim
and we listened
as the waves rhythmically
rode back and forth
yielding pleasantly hypnotic cries
against a warm and quiet shore
it was the preeminence of love
a carefully chosen time
solitude.

Have I Given You

Have I given you woe
and weeping eyes?
Have I given you beauty
in pure disguise?

Have I given you love
the best I've got?
Have I given you peace
in the midst of chaos?

Have I given you anger
to bring hurt and pain?
Have I given you disrespect
your heart to maim?

Have I given you hope
for what futures could bring?
Have I given you joy
or your life new meaning?

Have I given you
anything at all?
Have I given you
large or small?

Have I given you
the mystery of the sea?
Have I ... my love
given you me?

My Disease

My disease is not catching
but if you come real close
and touch my soul
you can feel it
running through my veins
often speaking
in monosyllabic phrases
about you and the world
around me.

My disease is not killing me
but gives me the will to live
and love the simplest treasures
in life like swinging in summer
sit-down dinners with my folks
or good old games of scrabble and spades
this is my disease.

It's taken over me and I keep fighting it
to fit a mold that America has thrown me
and sometimes I'm not quite sure
who "myself" is, but the disease
calls and comes for me
and the pain of it leaves me thinking
about tomorrow and how many of them
will be . . . my disease.

UNEQUALLY YOKED

Why are we unequally yoked
does my blackness and your whiteness
make us a joke?

Why are we unequally yoked
because your mom's a community leader
and mine gets beaten by the hands that feed her?

Why are we unequally yoked
because when I used Ebonics
you with flair and style spoke?

Why are we unequally yoked
because you're Catholic and I'm not
because your dad arrested mine for smoking pot?

Why are we unequally yoked
because you studied law
and I didn't use that time to study at all?

Why are we unequally yoked
because your Jesus is white
and mine is black?

Why are we are we . . .
unequally yoked
but so emotionally attached?

POETICIDE

Like flamboyant fleas
infesting a multicolored
carpet we wait
sometimes leaping
toward the heat
the mere movement
of a thing
in hopes that
we'll sink our sharp words
into the armpits and ears
of those who stand
before us
that they might
feel an itch or hurt
and be moved
even if minutely
because we exist
and are seldom seen
as artists
and next comes
the slaughter
of my son
and your daughter
the words
too much a bother
and we're slowly silenced.

Shop Wal-Mart For *Life*

I had spent what seemed only moments rummaging the aisles of Wal-Mart Super Center because my husband was headed for the field. He specifically penciled on the list one travel- sized toothpaste, baby wipes and sandwich bags, and I needed to shop for much more because it's what I like to do when he's away. It keeps me from having to drag the boys to Wal-Mart and deal with probing eyes that always leave me wondering if they want me to spank the whining child or time him out in house wares. I never really know. To be honest, I never care. So, it was going on ten, and I was basically skating down the aisles in hopes of not forgetting anything and in search of the things we needed: detergent, boneless chicken, milk, juice, fruit, cereal, paper towels, and pampers for the two-year-old who is still not potty trained. In one hour the basket is filled on top and beneath the basket, and I find a vacant line which is the main reason I love to shop Wal-Mart at night. A Swedish blonde in her thirties was at the checkout. We casually fell into conversation about her wanting to leave and work another job where she'd make eight dollars an hour, a place where she would "get a little more for working hard, long hours." I encouraged her, and her response was "but you're probably married to some rich man," and I almost laughed. Instead, I smiled and maybe even said "I wish." I told her that he wasn't rich, but that I couldn't complain. Well, I knew that I shouldn't because I work a part-time job teaching a few college students how to write, not to mention the fact that I write poetry and surf the internet all day for pleasure. I stay home with my kids, and here I stand with almost two hundred dollars worth of groceries for the week, paying with cash, my husband's cash. In her eyes, I might as well be rich. When she told me that she wrote poetry too, I smiled because we'd connected. She said next time I was in there she'd show me some. I invited her to check out my poetry site, another hobby of mine because I have the time, and again the level plane was broken. She didn't own a PC. She hadn't been able to afford one, so I encouraged her saying "all in good time." I halfway felt bad because my husband often reminds me that I'm blessed, and I know that I should be thankful for the things I have: a car, a house, two beautiful children whom I can be home with daily, a man who believes in and supports me, time to spend on hobbies, money to spend on half a basket of snacks, and I sit daily in a room with two computers - one for the house, and one for the road. Fortunate, blessed and stressed only when I give myself a reason. The Swedish blonde at the checkout reinforced the lesson. I walk daily in a wealth that I often don't remember that I possess. It's a secret that I keep from my own self because it's too easy, I guess, to want more not realizing that I already have more than I've ever had in my life. As I unloaded the bags from the cart and cranked the ignition to an almost ten-year-old, but paid for Honda, I was glad that I'd chosen aisle thirteen. It was a humbling experience in just moments at the checkout. I left Wal-Mart with something that's never been on my list, but I left with something that I needed most, a reminder.

CHARADES

looks like fun
sounds like knife
smells like blood
if you don't do it right
feels like love
runs on time
tastes like here and now
but never is
truly yours
or mine

Rights of Passage

Families don't realize the harm in
not passing on family information
because I don't really know what

my great grandfather looked like,
stood for, craved on Friday nights
or lived for. I'll never know because

no one passed it down. I remember
my great grandmother who could be
very quiet and mean at the same time,

a cute little old lady who
always got her point across in a few
words. If you pissed her off, the words

just got sharper and louder, but towards
the end, she didn't say much. I don't
think the cancer allowed her to feel

so she faded away slowly and
quietly without leaving a thing, no
words, no traditions, no life meanings

just a few acres of land in somebody's name
acres that everybody wanted to claim
and because living is never in vain

I guess I should cherish the white
and powdery biscuits she made to sop
molasses with, but I know she was more

than land, molasses, biscuits and a *sweet hello*
to her children and grandchildren, but no one tells
what I know exists, disrespecting rights of passage.

A Pharaoh's Heart

Sometimes
my inner voice tells me
that I'm too black
too down, too dismal
to the bound.

because
sometimes I'm the
pharaoh who will not
let those people
go.

and I find
the excruciating possibility
that it might be the world's fate
that I'm to wear a hardhat
beneath my breastplate.

so that good will be done,
that I might venture
into the white light of life
to look, think back
and know.

HAIKU 14
(when life is so uncertain)

live to love the life
just waiting to come alive
and be lived by you

Making Room

Old minds make plenty of sense
and they often utter wisely
ancient sayings of life and death
and I'm left sitting back and pensively pining
for answers to what is meant when they say
that room has to be made when babies come
or that dreams are likened to long *DE JA VUs*
and present day prophecies
but it's as simple as seasons coming and going
in line with the good sense of God
because what we are is life
and life is all about the science and psychology
of making room.

IF I TAUGHT YOU

If I taught you to walk
it was because I ran.

If I taught you to speak out
it was because I live in silence.

If I taught you to practice
it was because I wasted my talent.

If I taught you to save
it was because I spent it all.

If I taught you to pray
it was because I cursed.

If I taught you to endure
it was because I gave up.

If I taught you to forgive
it was because I held a grudge.

If I taught you to be saved
it was because I refused help.

If I taught you to love
it was because I hated.

If I taught you to live
it was because I died.

If I taught you . . .
it was because I did not learn.

You Taught Me

You taught me to walk
because it was the right way.

You taught me to speak out
because it would define me.

You taught me to practice
because it would make me better.

You taught me to save
because one day I would need.

You taught me to pray
because it would bring change.

You taught me to endure
because it would bring victory.

You taught me to forgive
because through it I'd gain peace.

You taught me to be saved
because it meant gaining eternal life.

You taught me to love
because it was God's greatest gift.

You taught me to live
because every life has a purpose.

You taught me . . .
because you learned.

Wishes for Grandfathers

I wish you dreams-come-true
on the wings of your appointed angel
and dirt roads paved in peace
on which to drive slower than slow.

I wish you a wealth of hope
to spend on you, your seed and the
generations of seeking souls
who crave Sunday afternoon talks.

I wish you love yielding admiration
and breezes on sunny days under
shady trees and grown kids who stop by
to see about you sipping a cool drink.

It Spoke to Me

It had a black cover, spine and back
and it spoke to me
of the beginning
and ending
of time as I'll ever
know it.
It spoke poetically
and eloquently of
a man whose words
were dipped in red
a man who fed a multitude
with two fish
and five loaves of bread
it had a black cover, spine and back
and it spoke to me.

Revelations

Running rampant is he
    contaminating the mainstream
infesting bloodlines over time
    singing praises to me.

Confusion is his name
    his dying wish to make me vain
and prophesy that beauty is a blessing
    adding fuel to the flame.

Recruits me in the valley still
    with bands of angels dressed to kill
wearing lying lips and halos of hell
    mendacity is his goodwill.

But true beauty descends as paradigm
    in balms, blessings and Sabbath wine
to prepare fallen feet for journeys
    of miracles and revelations over time.

RESTORATION

I sit and wait
or linger at the gate
but rest upon my fate
for You will restore me.

I am not forsaking Thee
or bringing evil upon me
but I'm living for the Trinity
because You are restoring me.

I don't look back now
or say *I made it somehow*
but know that it was Your vow
that saved and restored me.

I had never cried so
nor had I been made so low
but You never let me go
for Your love restored me.

My soul's in love and lifted up
Your blood endlessly fills my cup
and because I let You in to sup
with me, I am restored.

Twenty-Nine

Today I became a woman
for the eleventh time
and with the coming of midnight
came the screaming in my mind
It's coming . . . thirty's drumming
but today and twenty-nine are just fine,
just fine because I heard
some good preaching
did some good eating
spent some time with my boys
while God was just teaching
me to love me, my new number
the next level, another journey
a continuation of life, the celebration of a plight
from yesterday into today
and my awakenings in tomorrows
to behold a future, whether joy or sorrow
twenty-nine is just fine
because I'm living on Master time
and I'm given grace for my need, my seed
the little girl speaking to me
that I might walk carefully, calmly and with charisma
away from the tease
and into the beauty of the breeze and blue skies
and feel that I'm alive
that I might fall freely and fashionably
fathoming the abundance of articulate
words and phrases that fall on me like spiritual
embodiment and heart
that bring the deliverance that I need
faith to believe and the strength to conceive
of miracles and blessings for those standing in line
and I feel just fine . . . just fine I feel
at twenty-nine.

ADAM WHERE ARE YOU?

Where are you Adam
don't hide from me
I'll admit that I persuaded you
to eat of the forbidden tree

I just want you back
in my everyday life
don't you remember
God chose me for your wife

I know, I know Adam
you should have listened to God
but me and my bright ideas
just made your way hard

He told you and me
that we could have anything
but never to eat forbidden fruit
because it would change everything

But I love you Adam
please show yourself to me
we erred, the two of us
but we can still be free

In just one quick bite Adam
our world was rearranged
and that serpent who lied
will never be the same

Life in the garden
will never be as we knew it
but we still have a lot to live for
just come back, we'll get through it

Adam I will never make it
if you don't come back to me
God has predestined our seed
to live for eternity

my body's changing
my moods are not the same
Adam, can you hear me
come back and fulfill God's plan

The Garden's losing it's friendliness
the animals are no longer tame
they growl, roar and chase after me
as though life were a game

that apple was good
but only for a moment
who knew that one bite
would cause us such torment

I listened to that evil snake
and now look what we've done
it's bad, but without each other
life will never be any fun

I could give you back your rib
perhaps save you any further trouble
I'd do it Adam, I really would
to make you happy on the double

God had His reasons
for creating me too
but He made you first
so Adam, where are you?

I SEE YOU

I see you
instead of the warmth of sons
and I feel suddenly mistaken
for beauty when Luther's mellow melodies
don't send me leaping
into safe arms to love
and be loved sincerely.

I see you
when I stare stoically
into carefully carved eyes
feeling nothing
seeing nothing
just dark hues
of a blue that ain't blue.

When my soul lies prostrate
to problematic woes and means
when there's no spirit from which to glean
then I see you it seems.

When life's been twisted and torn
into misshapen space and time
when I walk as though my feet
have been confined
then I see you

Thinking Back

to what should have been
the happiest time in my life
wasn't
or was it

the day I
was born
graduated
high school
college
married
gave birth
to my first child
to my second son
to my writing
style

and since I can't remember
who's to really say
what aborted
babies did
or didn't feel
do or don't
remember
after the day
they
die

thinking back . .
would I remember
life?

WE'RE FALLING

The earth is sweating
with beautiful and talented
sisters and brothers
who play and write and sing.

And we're sliding down mountains
flowing in streams of consciousness
trickling down as memories from
the most high planes in life.

The earth is sweating
poets and writers. Some of us
are small, and our sizes take time to
fall into our places in the world.

But we will ... find a place
to wet and to wield our sacred
salt, the profound powers that be
pen and paper as we fall so freshly.

A Yard of Beauty

I had watched you
unintentionally really
and you brought beauty
to life
to live in
your garden

I never paused
to think what you
might be thinking
suicidal thoughts while bringing forth
such joy, such wonder
and with your hands

you were dying
while giving them life
to live, adorn and surround
your home
your heart
a pretty replacement
for you.

it was around five
in the afternoon
then we saw the lights
red, white and blue
they came for you
to rescue you
from what I'll never know.

and I wondered about it
and thought that hands just might
have to do a good deed
before they're allowed
to leave
or love
a yard of beauty.

A Blue Moon

falls from his lips
each time they part
and I find that my heart
hangs defenselessly
and stretched
from corner to corner
amongst stars
each time he utters
words

Choir Members

burning trials and tribulations melt
as melodic voices hail blessings come down

voices encircling
holding hands
lifting higher up.

the power of praise in medley
harmony and song
floating off chosen vocal chords
and trumpet lips
to waiting hearts,

seeking a glorious face
to magnify and exalt
in spirit and in truth.

THE BIG CHURCH

Everything is bigger at the big church.

the parked cars, the pews, the piano, the pulpit,
the preachers, the prayers, the praise dancers, the players

the teen-agers, the tongue talking, the tithing baskets,
the tithes, the tithers, the trials and the testimonies

Everything is bigger at the big church.

the suits, the songs, the sounds, the solos, the steeple
the spirit, the sinners, and the *say Amen's*

the men, the mothers, the microphones, the music
the marching, the melodies, the might and the ministries

Everything is bigger at the big church.

the caring, the clout, the clueless, the clubs,
the closet, the cures, the caresses, the crowds

the whiners, the watchers, the waiting, the whispers,
the worship, the wonder, the water, and the words.

Everything is bigger at the big church.

but Jesus stays the same
yesterday, today and forever

Dreams and Things

Every now and then
I dream a dream
of snakes
in all colors and sizes
for all occasions and surmises.

A snake in a dream
can only mean one thing
and I ask myself
"Why are these enemies
invading the privacy of my dreams?"

But these dreams of snakes
are dreams of life
and only God knows
when they'll show up
bringing strife.

As I dream these dreams
I try to remember
what the Word of God says
it might bruise my heel
but I can step on the snake's head.

Another Fall From Grace

My heart is broken and
the hands of time reversed
as we go back decades

each time I turn the channel
and see us half dressed
in embarrassing nakedness

in commercial minutes
we selfishly undo the
suffrage movement

and the years we fought
for freedom, equality
dignity and respect

today we give it back
each time we misrepresent
the gender, the politics

money happened . . .
to the struggle and we are
nonetheless blessed

but we've fallen from our grace
and finesse to the feet of
irreverent men again.

LIFE AFTER LOVE

Sometimes we cry colored tears
and they fall down cherished cheeks
when we kinetically kiss goodbye

while moments esoterically evolve
into years of yearning for melodramatic memories
of love given gracefully and gone awry

fail to hail the hypocrisy of happiness
that it might linger too long in private places
where the luxury of love no longer lives

send not the proud prowess of pity
to plead or make believe my stay
but let me flourish and fly freely away

leaving loquaciously upon this little life
collected and colorful remnants that remain
of life after love and cries of the insane.

THE DEEPEST PART OF ME

I think it's listening when I
vent, ramble, mumble or cry

Are you listening? . . . the reply
is always yes, yes, yes

I can't compete with the joy
of Sunday mornings and sports news

but I can turn cotton bed linens into
satin and safe havens

when I'm in complete touch
with the deepest part of me.

HAIKU 15-19
(epiphany)

15.

some lips that speak love
are as true as the kisses
bequeathed to an ass.

16.

lies have left lovers
questioning identity
in search of themselves

17.

never bleed a heart
that bleeds love, for the finish
yields long suffering

18.

I know what lust is
misplaced passion sentencing
innocence to life

19.

be faithful and know
when God sees crime committed
you reap what you sow

Too Young to Sip

I remember when the adults thought
we kids were too young to realize that they were
the world's biggest hypocrites.

It was never a secret that they loved the good life,
a drink here and there and the traditional Friday night
party. It was just their thing.

To live with one foot in the church and the other in
the world secretly, backsliding from earth to the core
nothing really, just on the way to hell without knowing.

It was just the occasional scotch and tonic some nights
nights they thought we were asleep or too wrapped up in TV
to notice their breaths, blood shot eyes and pure demise.

At those tender young ages even we knew hypocrites when
we saw them, so we did what grown folks say kids do best
we looked in the mirror, and we took a sip.

A Poem for Mama

on my mind
always
for you were there
when I couldn't think
for me
never forgetting
the life
the love
the lessons
you taught
the joy of Sunday meals
and late night talks
of country folk mishaps
and misfortunes
how you prayed
for me to be
somebody's woman
late to bed
early to rise
your hands at
hard labor
kneading dough
turning wheels
cooking meals
for eating
for teaching
for me.

A Phone Call

comes when you're unsuspecting
and into your ear flow words of need
and sometimes greed and misfortune,
and soon after you're writing . . .
a check, a letter, an apology
not knowing whether to laugh, cry or sigh --

cashing it, reading it, accepting it
or just forgetting all three like the neighbor
asking to borrow an egg that you'll never
get back even if you want it, gift or loan,
unsettled and seldom clear --

and this is you, the epitome of forgetfulness
and I am me, a subconscious and keeping
I forget and I don't forget--

ten years fly by, and I find myself still wondering
if you'll pause to see if I'm a keeper
of past memories or unsettled debts
you forget and you don't forget--

a phone call.

SCHOOLING

some people need schooling
and I'm not talking about the kind
you find in a book, school, college or university
but the kind that teaches overcoming adversity

we need to be taught to stand up and stand
we need to be taught to love our fellowman
we need to learn love, kindness and respect
we, as people, need to learn to pay our debt

we need the mother wit of mothers teaching women to be strong
and the strength of fathers training brothers for the storm
we need traditional families to strengthen a tie that binds
we need completion to live in these perilous times

it's sadly amazing when I see us on the street
ignorant of our self worth and living incomplete
when I see men abusing women because it's their choosing
this is what tells me that we still need schooling

some people need schooling
and I'm not talking about the kind
you find in a book, school, colleges or university
but that kind that teaches overcoming adversity

On Marriage

you ask me if you're the marrying kind
and I ask you how shall I ever know
answers to serious questions don't come overnight
but grow miraculously in the heart of a soul

and we've talked about what we think it means
commitment, trust, rings and things
but life will never let us forget
the tension and heat that marriages often beget

and will marriage cause you to lose or be lost
maybe, maybe not . . . it's a risk at all costs
don't look into me, but see the vision in you
in these modern times real marriages are few

minimize the cost of living
to find that you're the only heart giving
be forgiving . . . is what they say
but how many times in life, in a day?

I shall tie the knot but once
that is my solemn vow,
to be all that I can in marriage
find the true beauty in it somehow

God's Wrath is Coming Down

Mine eyes have seen the madness
of the catastrophe of life
it's tearing up the hearts and souls
of men on every side.

we live life from day to day
and hate each other because it pays
God's wrath is coming down.

mine eyes have seen the madness
of the catastrophe of life
it contaminates the blood in our veins
and nothing in life remains.

how much longer will we play the color game
when we're really all the same
God's wrath is coming down.

DEATH

Cast not your cares on me
because if I cared for you
I'd hasten my step to join you
quickly, arms folded in contentment,
I'd join you, sit down and sup with you

but you are not my friend
you are not the model of my kind
you are a new form of life that I fear
will not make me whole again
so I hide

from your creeping footsteps
and your night vision
that I may inhale a few more flecks
of love into my spirit
while you haphazardly collect my brethren.

Things That Bring Us Home

mama's sweet potato pie
weddings, funerals, a brother
or sister in love and trouble
daddy's near death experience
sadness
love past the point of no return
hate in disguise
family
reunions
things that bring us
home.

REASONS

We'll never get to know you
not even watch you tie your shoes.

Here we may not get to see you shine
but in our minds you rest with the Divine.

Miles away with angels you'll always be
in the hearts and souls of us throughout eternity.

But I'm happy that you came our way
to show us the reality of time and space.

God's reasoning is seldom understood, but always best
as we're left with memorable moments of feeling truly blessed.

The World is Coming to an End

I'm watching late night shows
of biblical doctrine and the news
and it's all adding up . . . for sure
the world is coming to an end.

It's what my grandmother used to say
whenever unbearable, painful, inhumane
sinful crimes led the way in newspaper
or TV headlines . . .

Today it's clearer, the day is nearer but
the words lead the way . . . while I read
of terrorists who can't be found, diseases
with no cure and fires that won't go out.

Haiku 20
(*trifling*)

it's like pure evil
when you let others pay for
the mistakes you make

Afghan Woman

I have come to know her only by TV
and lately, when I see her, I weep for
fear, for freedom, for the Afghan woman.

I stand in the shoes of a femininity with
rights and choices, I have arrived by the
grace of God through ancestors. So I

shed tears for her, she who can finally,
and maybe once again, wear her beauty
and feel her mind's freedom. She's been

denied priceless and precious moments
she's been denied the enhancements
education can bring. But maybe now,

from the abyss of war she'll rise victoriously
for herself, her children, her country and
live out the dreams she's dreamed. We are

similar. She is woman. I am woman, and
we desire to be made whole, to live lives of
free will and chosen paths of our destinies.

I see her, with covered face and body, just
moments after having sold her child that they
both might eat, after living in fear of savagery.

I see her pain. I am called by her name, and
I cry because my face was also covered, my ankles
whipped, and my books taken away from me.

I live in fear and pray for peace each time TV brings
her near. She is here, I am there, and across
the miles I've come to share her pain.

Chaos

From the depths of a mean spirited world
where love realizes hate becomes us
and tears away, just eats away at us
souls rot to the core
of human beings
and I, with my bible reading self,
stand too confused about what to make of this
the here and now
the afterlife
as I'm faced with fears of immortality
red blood in blue veins
running on time
while life stands still at the creation of war
and the cremation of peace
with books, words, ethics,
money and motions,
potions, philosophies,
solutions and sayings
the earth spins, minute by minute
into one sordid and confusing ideology
to greet the dutiful chosen who have challenged life
defining it, maligning it, pretending to give it
then taking it away
those tongues of fire that preach to us
without leading us . . . souls along the way
and I stand so . . . commanded by thoughts
of living

--in today's chaos--

without a soul.

C Words

I wish I knew
why we put faith in men we see
those who often fail us cold heartedly

we say
why trust in a God we cannot see
to lead us into our destiny

but all the while
it's man that we cannot see
who stands before us as one, not three

and God
his loving presence comes three-fold
to fulfill His promise and His covenant keep

salvation
it's never been about challenges
but always about commitment

Dying in My Sleep

I had often fathomed
dying in my sleep

and if I had to go
I thought it the best way

but last night, in the midst of
chaotic slumber, I fathomed waking

before dying because my head
had grown horns, two crowns of thorns

hell had come to me and for me
invading my face, my space

horror surrounded me, filled me
and the world laughed at my misery

while time stood still doing nothing
no chants of exorcism, no prayer

no healing, nothing, just me
dying in my sleep.

GIRL INTERRUPTED

by a
shallow
mind

repeating a
cycle

over
and
over

again

a *taking*
    a *raping*
        a *mistaking*

the
silence
for
c
o
n
s
e
n
t

My America

these lines really depend on me
the day of the week
and the mood I'm in

because this could take a while
the way I feel, the love I have,
the hurt inside of me

on being American
a black American
a female American

it's no ordinary love
or the things I've seen
my ancestors hauled away

from their Kings and Queens
to mix and mingle under the
sound and fury of whips

to be rebuked and scorned
and kissed by white lips
hence, the skin I'm in

runs deep, way back to the
Nile, a river that runs deep
in me and my American seed

we came, against our wills
with soil to till, cotton to pick
and clothes to stitch

this is my mother's America
my America, my children's
America . . . it is ours

and up from slavery the black
man did rise in search of the
great Compromise . . .

once bound, now free
but without rights and equality
what kind of people would we be

in a world of injustice, a sick society
no kind of woman, no kind of man
thank God some of us had a plan

the will, the mind, the need
to be free and treated fairly
dark skin clean as skin could be

mistreated because ignorance was free
to roam and manifest in blue veins
reduced to calling black folks names

It's America, my mother's America
my America and the America of my seed
but not the America that we need

Not yet. Not yet. Not yet you see
because this is an America
traveling light-years to be free.

My America.

You'll Never Find You

You'll never find you
between a woman's thighs
or the hazel green of her eyes.

You'll never find you
underneath a Sunday hat
or a splendid home and welcome mat.

You'll never find you
hanging on office walls
or at your mother's beck and call.

You'll never find you
in the fleshy filaments of skin
or in the balms of blood and kin.

You'll never find you
not here or there
but look you must, everywhere.

SACRED PLACES TURNED INSIDE OUT

Satan, get behind me. Don't place
our youngest boys on your laps
to lip kiss them into glory.

Your hands hold evil oils which soothe
and bless a sinful spirit, those that
tarry so far from Heaven's anointing.

You sprinkle your holy waters
on heads of babes with hopes of
lying them down to steal waters

That run fresh and seek God's face
through you, thus abandoning the
utmost call for New Testament Passion

In the name of sick psychosis. I pray
that saint denied souls can hold out in the
rapture of sacred places turned inside out.

Sudden Feelings, Never Lasting

breaking out . . . in hives
an all day dream of itches to scratch
welts of love, loneliness and confusion
give me some cool to ease the pain
give me some cool . . . call my name.

night comes creeping all around
to serenade my soul with darkness
because it's cleansing time
it's mending time for lovers in the night
because mornings take our breath away.

like chivalry in search of destiny
we set sail for suns to set
with outstretched hands and hearts
to greet resentment with resilience
and once more be better for it.

Deliverance II

Father remove this cup from me
the curse of lies, lust and trickery
repeat after me and we shall see
if the promise of God deliverance be.

Life is laced with seduction and surprise
and the ways we're seen through others' eyes
to err is human -- the great disguise
leaving scholars the world over to philosophize.

Come death to do us thy diligent deed
carrying crowns of glory upon thy steed
for we fail to call upon thee but for greed
having chosen the abyss from which to feed.

We utter in want "thy will be done"
without accepting the reality of the Son
one's left to live not as the chosen one
in denial that the Truth would ever come.

Father remove this cup from me
selfishness, disobedience and disbelief
intertwine within our spirits for the world to see
a love that's lasting, unconditional and free.

NOT MY NATION, NOT MY BELIEFS

I'm in America . . .
yet I feel an omnipresence about me
for I am a lot of people in many places.
I am everywhere every moment
Afghanistan, Bali, Kandahar . . . you name it.
I am everywhere . . .
witnessing the unanticipated results of a terrorism
that daily lifts its suicidal head to stare and tear me down
and I hate the look it gives to me.

I'm in America
yet I feel an overwhelming omniscience
for I know these people in these places
that they stand to reap the wrath of war not God
they will suffer the revenge of many nations
against one, against few
in the name of terrorism
a world at war for peace
and I weep for the unified souls
so quickly turning their cheeks
right then left . . . continual

I'm in America, and I am not
yet I feel the attack
the peace keeper's might
the martyr
the non-George Bush-and-his-Congress cheeks
stand rosy red, tears streaming down
mouth ajar. . . uttering

please don't . . . for it is I . . . who will pay the price

not my nation
not my belief
me.

WHERE TO NOW AMERICA?

Where to now America
do we avenge the perished souls
set an example of a peaceful nation
listen to God, pray for solace
play politics or wage war?

Where to now America
do we tear up lands and tear down walls
then strive to build them back up again
do we hide behind creeds and patriotism
or press on with greed and cynicism?

Where to now America
your intentions are unclear
while a world fears the end is near
are you merely a chess player with pieces
moving countries and men across borders?

Where to now America
to humanity, to money, to leaders or to citizens
to east, to west, to intelligence or to ignorance
to salvation, to destruction, to right or to wrong
to honor, to love, to peace or to war?

Where to now . . . America?

THE MAN IN MY LIFE

There used to be a time when I couldn't sleep, couldn't eat
and thinking about you just made me weak

I couldn't close my eyes nor open my mouth
thought I'd lose you in the process, somehow

It's funny how a fool in love is
wanting nothing in life but to be his

I've matured way past life's maturity
and found out that you mean so much to me

Now today I stand, a whole new woman
married to the man I spent my life following

No regrets, still in love until the day I die
because you're a real man . . . and I can't lie.

HAIKU 21
(*book review*)

you just read my mind
now I'm anxious for you to
tell me what I think

IMMACULATE PERCEPTIONS
Poems by Latorial Faison

Look for this book online at

Amazon.com

Bring Latorial Faison's books to your local
Book stores and libraries

IMMACULATE PERCEPTIONS

SECRETS OF MY SOUL

Visit Latorial Faison Online
www.latorialfaison.com

Cross Keys Press
crosskeyspress@aol.com

Made in the USA
Columbia, SC
14 December 2022